TENNIS SCORE BOOK

Are you enjoying this awesome book?

If so, please leave us a review. We are very interested in your feedback to create even better products for you to enjoy soon.

Shopping for Tennis Score Books can be fun. Go to our page on Amazon http://bit.ly/amazing-notebooks or scan the QR code below to see all of our awesome and creative products!

Thank you very much!

Amazing Tennis Score Books
www.amazing-notebooks.com

TENNIS SCORE BOOK

THIS JOURNAL BELONGS TO

Name . . . .

Phone . . . .

Email . . . .

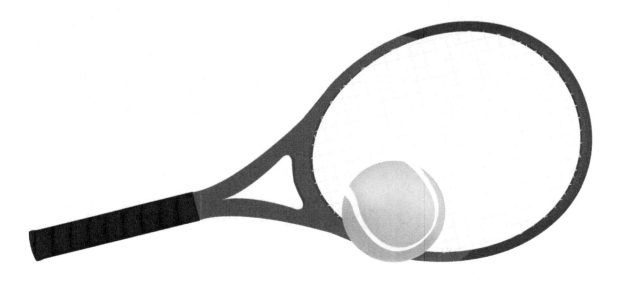

TENNIS SCORE SHEET

DATE	PLACE	TIME	WEATHER	COURT CONDITIONS	

HOME	LEAGUE	SEASON	OPPONENT	LEAGUE	SEASON

SINGLES — RECORDS — MATCH SCORES

No	HOME	H	O	OPPONENT	SET 1	SET 2	SET 3	WINNER
1								
2								
3								
4								
5								
6								

DOUBLES — RECORDS — MATCH SCORES

No	HOME	H	O	OPPONENT	SET 1	SET 2	SET 3	WINNER
1								
2								
3								

TOTALS

TENNIS SCORE SHEET

DATE	PLACE	TIME	WEATHER	COURT CONDITIONS	
HOME	LEAGUE	SEASON	OPPONENT	LEAGUE	SEASON

SINGLES — RECORDS — MATCH SCORES

No	HOME	H	O	OPPONENT	SET 1	SET 2	SET 3	WINNER
1								
2								
3								
4								
5								
6								

DOUBLES — RECORDS — MATCH SCORES

No	HOME	H	O	OPPONENT	SET 1	SET 2	SET 3	WINNER
1								
2								
3								

TOTALS

TENNIS SCORE SHEET

DATE	PLACE	TIME	WEATHER	COURT CONDITIONS	
HOME	LEAGUE	SEASON	OPPONENT	LEAGUE	SEASON

SINGLES — RECORDS — MATCH SCORES

No	HOME	H	O	OPPONENT	SET 1	SET 2	SET 3	WINNER
1								
2								
3								
4								
5								
6								

DOUBLES — RECORDS — MATCH SCORES

No	HOME	H	O	OPPONENT	SET 1	SET 2	SET 3	WINNER
1								
2								
3								

TOTALS			

TENNIS SCORE SHEET

DATE	PLACE	TIME	WEATHER	COURT CONDITIONS	
HOME	LEAGUE	SEASON	OPPONENT	LEAGUE	SEASON

SINGLES		RECORDS			MATCH SCORES			
No	**HOME**	**H**	**O**	**OPPONENT**	**SET 1**	**SET 2**	**SET 3**	**WINNER**
1								
2								
3								
4								
5								
6								

DOUBLES		RECORDS			MATCH SCORES			
No	**HOME**	**H**	**O**	**OPPONENT**	**SET 1**	**SET 2**	**SET 3**	**WINNER**
1								
2								
3								

TOTALS

TENNIS SCORE SHEET

DATE	PLACE	TIME	WEATHER	COURT CONDITIONS	

HOME	LEAGUE	SEASON	OPPONENT	LEAGUE	SEASON

SINGLES

No	HOME	RECORDS		OPPONENT	MATCH SCORES			
		H	O		SET 1	SET 2	SET 3	WINNER
1								
2								
3								
4								
5								
6								

DOUBLES

No	HOME	RECORDS		OPPONENT	MATCH SCORES			
		H	O		SET 1	SET 2	SET 3	WINNER
1								
2								
3								

TOTALS			

TENNIS SCORE SHEET

DATE	PLACE	TIME	WEATHER	COURT CONDITIONS	
HOME	**LEAGUE**	**SEASON**	**OPPONENT**	**LEAGUE**	**SEASON**

SINGLES — RECORDS — MATCH SCORES

No	HOME	H	O	OPPONENT	SET 1	SET 2	SET 3	WINNER
1								
2								
3								
4								
5								
6								

DOUBLES — RECORDS — MATCH SCORES

No	HOME	H	O	OPPONENT	SET 1	SET 2	SET 3	WINNER
1								
2								
3								

TOTALS

TENNIS SCORE SHEET

DATE	PLACE	TIME	WEATHER	COURT CONDITIONS	
HOME	**LEAGUE**	**SEASON**	**OPPONENT**	**LEAGUE**	**SEASON**

SINGLES

No	HOME	RECORDS H	RECORDS O	OPPONENT	SET 1	SET 2	SET 3	WINNER
1								
2								
3								
4								
5								
6								

DOUBLES

No	HOME	RECORDS H	RECORDS O	OPPONENT	SET 1	SET 2	SET 3	WINNER
1								
2								
3								

			TOTALS			

TENNIS SCORE SHEET

DATE	PLACE	TIME	WEATHER	COURT CONDITIONS	
HOME	LEAGUE	SEASON	OPPONENT	LEAGUE	SEASON

SINGLES — RECORDS — MATCH SCORES

No	HOME	H	O	OPPONENT	SET 1	SET 2	SET 3	WINNER
1								
2								
3								
4								
5								
6								

DOUBLES — RECORDS — MATCH SCORES

No	HOME	H	O	OPPONENT	SET 1	SET 2	SET 3	WINNER
1								
2								
3								

TOTALS

TENNIS SCORE SHEET

DATE	PLACE	TIME	WEATHER	COURT CONDITIONS	
HOME	LEAGUE	SEASON	OPPONENT	LEAGUE	SEASON

SINGLES — RECORDS — MATCH SCORES

No	HOME	H	O	OPPONENT	SET 1	SET 2	SET 3	WINNER
1								
2								
3								
4								
5								
6								

DOUBLES — RECORDS — MATCH SCORES

No	HOME	H	O	OPPONENT	SET 1	SET 2	SET 3	WINNER
1								
2								
3								

TOTALS

TENNIS SCORE SHEET

DATE	PLACE	TIME	WEATHER	COURT CONDITIONS	
HOME	LEAGUE	SEASON	OPPONENT	LEAGUE	SEASON

SINGLES

No	HOME	RECORDS H	RECORDS O	OPPONENT	SET 1	SET 2	SET 3	WINNER
1								
2								
3								
4								
5								
6								

DOUBLES

No	HOME	RECORDS H	RECORDS O	OPPONENT	SET 1	SET 2	SET 3	WINNER
1								
2								
3								

TOTALS

TENNIS SCORE SHEET

DATE	PLACE	TIME	WEATHER	COURT CONDITIONS	
HOME	LEAGUE	SEASON	OPPONENT	LEAGUE	SEASON

SINGLES

No	HOME	H	O	OPPONENT	SET 1	SET 2	SET 3	WINNER
			RECORDS			MATCH SCORES		
1								
2								
3								
4								
5								
6								

DOUBLES

No	HOME	H	O	OPPONENT	SET 1	SET 2	SET 3	WINNER
			RECORDS			MATCH SCORES		
1								
2								
3								

TOTALS

TENNIS SCORE SHEET

DATE	PLACE	TIME	WEATHER	COURT CONDITIONS	
HOME	LEAGUE	SEASON	OPPONENT	LEAGUE	SEASON

SINGLES — RECORDS — MATCH SCORES

No	HOME	H	O	OPPONENT	SET 1	SET 2	SET 3	WINNER
1								
2								
3								
4								
5								
6								

DOUBLES — RECORDS — MATCH SCORES

No	HOME	H	O	OPPONENT	SET 1	SET 2	SET 3	WINNER
1								
2								
3								

TOTALS

TENNIS SCORE SHEET

DATE	PLACE	TIME	WEATHER	COURT CONDITIONS	
HOME	LEAGUE	SEASON	OPPONENT	LEAGUE	SEASON

SINGLES — RECORDS — MATCH SCORES

No	HOME	H	O	OPPONENT	SET 1	SET 2	SET 3	WINNER
1								
2								
3								
4								
5								
6								

DOUBLES — RECORDS — MATCH SCORES

No	HOME	H	O	OPPONENT	SET 1	SET 2	SET 3	WINNER
1								
2								
3								

TOTALS

TENNIS SCORE SHEET

DATE	PLACE	TIME	WEATHER	COURT CONDITIONS	
HOME	**LEAGUE**	**SEASON**	**OPPONENT**	**LEAGUE**	**SEASON**

SINGLES — RECORDS — MATCH SCORES

No	HOME	H	O	OPPONENT	SET 1	SET 2	SET 3	WINNER
1								
2								
3								
4								
5								
6								

DOUBLES — RECORDS — MATCH SCORES

No	HOME	H	O	OPPONENT	SET 1	SET 2	SET 3	WINNER
1								
2								
3								

| | | | | | **TOTALS** | | | |

TENNIS SCORE SHEET

DATE	PLACE	TIME	WEATHER	COURT CONDITIONS	

HOME	LEAGUE	SEASON	OPPONENT	LEAGUE	SEASON

SINGLES — RECORDS — MATCH SCORES

No	HOME	H	O	OPPONENT	SET 1	SET 2	SET 3	WINNER
1								
2								
3								
4								
5								
6								

DOUBLES — RECORDS — MATCH SCORES

No	HOME	H	O	OPPONENT	SET 1	SET 2	SET 3	WINNER
1								
2								
3								

	TOTALS			

TENNIS SCORE SHEET

DATE	PLACE	TIME	WEATHER	COURT CONDITIONS	
HOME	LEAGUE	SEASON	OPPONENT	LEAGUE	SEASON

SINGLES — RECORDS — MATCH SCORES

No	HOME	H	O	OPPONENT	SET 1	SET 2	SET 3	WINNER
1								
2								
3								
4								
5								
6								

DOUBLES — RECORDS — MATCH SCORES

No	HOME	H	O	OPPONENT	SET 1	SET 2	SET 3	WINNER
1								
2								
3								

TOTALS

TENNIS SCORE SHEET

DATE	PLACE	TIME	WEATHER	COURT CONDITIONS	
HOME	**LEAGUE**	**SEASON**	**OPPONENT**	**LEAGUE**	**SEASON**

SINGLES

No	HOME	RECORDS H	RECORDS O	OPPONENT	SET 1	SET 2	SET 3	WINNER
1								
2								
3								
4								
5								
6								

RECORDS / MATCH SCORES

DOUBLES

No	HOME	RECORDS H	RECORDS O	OPPONENT	SET 1	SET 2	SET 3	WINNER
1								
2								
3								

RECORDS / MATCH SCORES

TOTALS

TENNIS SCORE SHEET

DATE	PLACE	TIME	WEATHER	COURT CONDITIONS	
HOME	**LEAGUE**	**SEASON**	**OPPONENT**	**LEAGUE**	**SEASON**

SINGLES — RECORDS — MATCH SCORES

No	HOME	H	O	OPPONENT	SET 1	SET 2	SET 3	WINNER
1								
2								
3								
4								
5								
6								

DOUBLES — RECORDS — MATCH SCORES

No	HOME	H	O	OPPONENT	SET 1	SET 2	SET 3	WINNER
1								
2								
3								

TOTALS

TENNIS SCORE SHEET

DATE	PLACE	TIME	WEATHER	COURT CONDITIONS	
HOME	**LEAGUE**	**SEASON**	**OPPONENT**	**LEAGUE**	**SEASON**

SINGLES — RECORDS — MATCH SCORES

No	HOME	H	O	OPPONENT	SET 1	SET 2	SET 3	WINNER
1								
2								
3								
4								
5								
6								

DOUBLES — RECORDS — MATCH SCORES

No	HOME	H	O	OPPONENT	SET 1	SET 2	SET 3	WINNER
1								
2								
3								

TOTALS

TENNIS SCORE SHEET

DATE	PLACE	TIME	WEATHER	COURT CONDITIONS	
HOME	**LEAGUE**	**SEASON**	**OPPONENT**	**LEAGUE**	**SEASON**

SINGLES

No	HOME	H	O	OPPONENT	SET 1	SET 2	SET 3	WINNER
1								
2								
3								
4								
5								
6								

RECORDS · MATCH SCORES

DOUBLES

No	HOME	H	O	OPPONENT	SET 1	SET 2	SET 3	WINNER
1								
2								
3								

RECORDS · MATCH SCORES

TOTALS

TENNIS SCORE SHEET

DATE	PLACE	TIME	WEATHER	COURT CONDITIONS	

HOME	LEAGUE	SEASON	OPPONENT	LEAGUE	SEASON

SINGLES — RECORDS — MATCH SCORES

No	HOME	H	O	OPPONENT	SET 1	SET 2	SET 3	WINNER
1								
2								
3								
4								
5								
6								

DOUBLES — RECORDS — MATCH SCORES

No	HOME	H	O	OPPONENT	SET 1	SET 2	SET 3	WINNER
1								
2								
3								

TOTALS

TENNIS SCORE SHEET

DATE	PLACE	TIME	WEATHER	COURT CONDITIONS	
HOME	LEAGUE	SEASON	OPPONENT	LEAGUE	SEASON

SINGLES — RECORDS — MATCH SCORES

No	HOME	H	O	OPPONENT	SET 1	SET 2	SET 3	WINNER
1								
2								
3								
4								
5								
6								

DOUBLES — RECORDS — MATCH SCORES

No	HOME	H	O	OPPONENT	SET 1	SET 2	SET 3	WINNER
1								
2								
3								

TOTALS

TENNIS SCORE SHEET

DATE	PLACE	TIME	WEATHER	COURT CONDITIONS	
HOME	LEAGUE	SEASON	OPPONENT	LEAGUE	SEASON

🎾 SINGLES — RECORDS — MATCH SCORES

No	HOME	H	O	OPPONENT	SET 1	SET 2	SET 3	WINNER
1								
2								
3								
4								
5								
6								

🎾 DOUBLES — RECORDS — MATCH SCORES

No	HOME	H	O	OPPONENT	SET 1	SET 2	SET 3	WINNER
1								
2								
3								

TOTALS

TENNIS SCORE SHEET

DATE	PLACE	TIME	WEATHER	COURT CONDITIONS	
HOME	LEAGUE	SEASON	OPPONENT	LEAGUE	SEASON

SINGLES — RECORDS — MATCH SCORES

No	HOME	H	O	OPPONENT	SET 1	SET 2	SET 3	WINNER
1								
2								
3								
4								
5								
6								

DOUBLES — RECORDS — MATCH SCORES

No	HOME	H	O	OPPONENT	SET 1	SET 2	SET 3	WINNER
1								
2								
3								

TOTALS

TENNIS SCORE SHEET

DATE	PLACE	TIME	WEATHER	COURT CONDITIONS	
HOME	LEAGUE	SEASON	OPPONENT	LEAGUE	SEASON

SINGLES — RECORDS — MATCH SCORES

No	HOME	H	O	OPPONENT	SET 1	SET 2	SET 3	WINNER
1								
2								
3								
4								
5								
6								

DOUBLES — RECORDS — MATCH SCORES

No	HOME	H	O	OPPONENT	SET 1	SET 2	SET 3	WINNER
1								
2								
3								

TOTALS

TENNIS SCORE SHEET

DATE	PLACE	TIME	WEATHER	COURT CONDITIONS	
HOME	**LEAGUE**	**SEASON**	**OPPONENT**	**LEAGUE**	**SEASON**

SINGLES — RECORDS — MATCH SCORES

No	HOME	H	O	OPPONENT	SET 1	SET 2	SET 3	WINNER
1								
2								
3								
4								
5								
6								

DOUBLES — RECORDS — MATCH SCORES

No	HOME	H	O	OPPONENT	SET 1	SET 2	SET 3	WINNER
1								
2								
3								

TOTALS

TENNIS SCORE SHEET

DATE	PLACE	TIME	WEATHER	COURT CONDITIONS	
HOME	LEAGUE	SEASON	OPPONENT	LEAGUE	SEASON

🎾 SINGLES — RECORDS — MATCH SCORES

No	HOME	H	O	OPPONENT	SET 1	SET 2	SET 3	WINNER
1								
2								
3								
4								
5								
6								

🎾 DOUBLES — RECORDS — MATCH SCORES

No	HOME	H	O	OPPONENT	SET 1	SET 2	SET 3	WINNER
1								
2								
3								

	TOTALS			

TENNIS SCORE SHEET

DATE	PLACE	TIME	WEATHER	COURT CONDITIONS	
HOME	**LEAGUE**	**SEASON**	**OPPONENT**	**LEAGUE**	**SEASON**

SINGLES

No	HOME	RECORDS H	O	OPPONENT	SET 1	SET 2	SET 3	WINNER
1								
2								
3								
4								
5								
6								

RECORDS · *MATCH SCORES*

DOUBLES

No	HOME	RECORDS H	O	OPPONENT	SET 1	SET 2	SET 3	WINNER
1								
2								
3								

RECORDS · *MATCH SCORES*

TOTALS

TENNIS SCORE SHEET

DATE	PLACE	TIME	WEATHER	COURT CONDITIONS	
HOME	**LEAGUE**	**SEASON**	**OPPONENT**	**LEAGUE**	**SEASON**

SINGLES

No	HOME	RECORDS H	RECORDS O	OPPONENT	SET 1	SET 2	SET 3	WINNER
1								
2								
3								
4								
5								
6								

MATCH SCORES

DOUBLES

No	HOME	RECORDS H	RECORDS O	OPPONENT	SET 1	SET 2	SET 3	WINNER
1								
2								
3								

MATCH SCORES

TOTALS

TENNIS SCORE SHEET

DATE	PLACE	TIME	WEATHER	COURT CONDITIONS	

HOME	LEAGUE	SEASON	OPPONENT	LEAGUE	SEASON

SINGLES · RECORDS · MATCH SCORES

No	HOME	H	O	OPPONENT	SET 1	SET 2	SET 3	WINNER
1								
2								
3								
4								
5								
6								

DOUBLES · RECORDS · MATCH SCORES

No	HOME	H	O	OPPONENT	SET 1	SET 2	SET 3	WINNER
1								
2								
3								

TOTALS

TENNIS SCORE SHEET

DATE	PLACE	TIME	WEATHER	COURT CONDITIONS	

HOME	LEAGUE	SEASON	OPPONENT	LEAGUE	SEASON

SINGLES

No	HOME		RECORDS		OPPONENT		MATCH SCORES			
		H	O			SET 1	SET 2	SET 3	WINNER	
1										
2										
3										
4										
5										
6										

DOUBLES

No	HOME	H	O	OPPONENT	SET 1	SET 2	SET 3	WINNER
1								
2								
3								

TOTALS

TENNIS SCORE SHEET

DATE	PLACE	TIME	WEATHER	COURT CONDITIONS	
HOME	LEAGUE	SEASON	OPPONENT	LEAGUE	SEASON

SINGLES — RECORDS — MATCH SCORES

No	HOME	H	O	OPPONENT	SET 1	SET 2	SET 3	WINNER
1								
2								
3								
4								
5								
6								

DOUBLES — RECORDS — MATCH SCORES

No	HOME	H	O	OPPONENT	SET 1	SET 2	SET 3	WINNER
1								
2								
3								

TOTALS

TENNIS SCORE SHEET

DATE	PLACE	TIME	WEATHER	COURT CONDITIONS	

HOME	LEAGUE	SEASON	OPPONENT	LEAGUE	SEASON

SINGLES — RECORDS — MATCH SCORES

No	HOME	H	O	OPPONENT	SET 1	SET 2	SET 3	WINNER
1								
2								
3								
4								
5								
6								

DOUBLES — RECORDS — MATCH SCORES

No	HOME	H	O	OPPONENT	SET 1	SET 2	SET 3	WINNER
1								
2								
3								

		TOTALS		

TENNIS SCORE SHEET

DATE	PLACE	TIME	WEATHER	COURT CONDITIONS	
HOME	**LEAGUE**	**SEASON**	**OPPONENT**	**LEAGUE**	**SEASON**

SINGLES — RECORDS — MATCH SCORES

No	HOME	H	O	OPPONENT	SET 1	SET 2	SET 3	WINNER
1								
2								
3								
4								
5								
6								

DOUBLES — RECORDS — MATCH SCORES

No	HOME	H	O	OPPONENT	SET 1	SET 2	SET 3	WINNER
1								
2								
3								

TOTALS

TENNIS SCORE SHEET

DATE	PLACE	TIME	WEATHER	COURT CONDITIONS	
HOME	LEAGUE	SEASON	OPPONENT	LEAGUE	SEASON

SINGLES

No	HOME	RECORDS		OPPONENT	MATCH SCORES			
		H	O		SET 1	SET 2	SET 3	WINNER
1								
2								
3								
4								
5								
6								

DOUBLES

No	HOME	RECORDS		OPPONENT	MATCH SCORES			
		H	O		SET 1	SET 2	SET 3	WINNER
1								
2								
3								

	TOTALS		

TENNIS SCORE SHEET

DATE	PLACE	TIME	WEATHER	COURT CONDITIONS	
HOME	**LEAGUE**	**SEASON**	**OPPONENT**	**LEAGUE**	**SEASON**

SINGLES

No	HOME	RECORDS H	RECORDS O	OPPONENT	SET 1	SET 2	SET 3	WINNER
1								
2								
3								
4								
5								
6								

DOUBLES

No	HOME	RECORDS H	RECORDS O	OPPONENT	SET 1	SET 2	SET 3	WINNER
1								
2								
3								

TOTALS

TENNIS SCORE SHEET

DATE	PLACE	TIME	WEATHER	COURT CONDITIONS	

HOME	LEAGUE	SEASON	OPPONENT	LEAGUE	SEASON

SINGLES

No	HOME	RECORDS H	O	OPPONENT	SET 1	SET 2	SET 3	WINNER
1								
2								
3								
4								
5								
6								

DOUBLES

No	HOME	RECORDS H	O	OPPONENT	SET 1	SET 2	SET 3	WINNER
1								
2								
3								

TOTALS

TENNIS SCORE SHEET

DATE	PLACE	TIME	WEATHER	COURT CONDITIONS	
HOME	LEAGUE	SEASON	OPPONENT	LEAGUE	SEASON

SINGLES   RECORDS   MATCH SCORES

No	HOME	H	O	OPPONENT	SET 1	SET 2	SET 3	WINNER
1								
2								
3								
4								
5								
6								

DOUBLES   RECORDS   MATCH SCORES

No	HOME	H	O	OPPONENT	SET 1	SET 2	SET 3	WINNER
1								
2								
3								

TOTALS

TENNIS SCORE SHEET

DATE	PLACE	TIME	WEATHER	COURT CONDITIONS	
HOME	LEAGUE	SEASON	OPPONENT	LEAGUE	SEASON

SINGLES — RECORDS — MATCH SCORES

No	HOME	H	O	OPPONENT	SET 1	SET 2	SET 3	WINNER
1								
2								
3								
4								
5								
6								

DOUBLES — RECORDS — MATCH SCORES

No	HOME	H	O	OPPONENT	SET 1	SET 2	SET 3	WINNER
1								
2								
3								

TOTALS

TENNIS SCORE SHEET

DATE	PLACE	TIME	WEATHER	COURT CONDITIONS	
HOME	LEAGUE	SEASON	OPPONENT	LEAGUE	SEASON

SINGLES — RECORDS — MATCH SCORES

No	HOME	H	O	OPPONENT	SET 1	SET 2	SET 3	WINNER
1								
2								
3								
4								
5								
6								

DOUBLES — RECORDS — MATCH SCORES

No	HOME	H	O	OPPONENT	SET 1	SET 2	SET 3	WINNER
1								
2								
3								

TOTALS

TENNIS SCORE SHEET

DATE	PLACE	TIME	WEATHER	COURT CONDITIONS	
HOME	LEAGUE	SEASON	OPPONENT	LEAGUE	SEASON

SINGLES — RECORDS — MATCH SCORES

No	HOME	H	O	OPPONENT	SET 1	SET 2	SET 3	WINNER
1								
2								
3								
4								
5								
6								

DOUBLES — RECORDS — MATCH SCORES

No	HOME	H	O	OPPONENT	SET 1	SET 2	SET 3	WINNER
1								
2								
3								

TOTALS

TENNIS SCORE SHEET

DATE	PLACE	TIME	WEATHER	COURT CONDITIONS	
HOME	LEAGUE	SEASON	OPPONENT	LEAGUE	SEASON

🎾 SINGLES — RECORDS — MATCH SCORES

No	HOME	H	O	OPPONENT	SET 1	SET 2	SET 3	WINNER
1								
2								
3								
4								
5								
6								

🎾 DOUBLES — RECORDS — MATCH SCORES

No	HOME	H	O	OPPONENT	SET 1	SET 2	SET 3	WINNER
1								
2								
3								

TOTALS

TENNIS SCORE SHEET

DATE	PLACE	TIME	WEATHER	COURT CONDITIONS	
HOME	LEAGUE	SEASON	OPPONENT	LEAGUE	SEASON

SINGLES — RECORDS — MATCH SCORES

No	HOME	H	O	OPPONENT	SET 1	SET 2	SET 3	WINNER
1								
2								
3								
4								
5								
6								

DOUBLES — RECORDS — MATCH SCORES

No	HOME	H	O	OPPONENT	SET 1	SET 2	SET 3	WINNER
1								
2								
3								

TOTALS

TENNIS SCORE SHEET

DATE	PLACE	TIME	WEATHER	COURT CONDITIONS	
HOME	**LEAGUE**	**SEASON**	**OPPONENT**	**LEAGUE**	**SEASON**

SINGLES — RECORDS — MATCH SCORES

No	HOME	H	O	OPPONENT	SET 1	SET 2	SET 3	WINNER
1								
2								
3								
4								
5								
6								

DOUBLES — RECORDS — MATCH SCORES

No	HOME	H	O	OPPONENT	SET 1	SET 2	SET 3	WINNER
1								
2								
3								

TOTALS

TENNIS SCORE SHEET

DATE	PLACE	TIME	WEATHER	COURT CONDITIONS	
HOME	LEAGUE	SEASON	OPPONENT	LEAGUE	SEASON

🎾 SINGLES — RECORDS — MATCH SCORES

No	HOME	H	O	OPPONENT	SET 1	SET 2	SET 3	WINNER
1								
2								
3								
4								
5								
6								

🎾 DOUBLES — RECORDS — MATCH SCORES

No	HOME	H	O	OPPONENT	SET 1	SET 2	SET 3	WINNER
1								
2								
3								

TOTALS

TENNIS SCORE SHEET

DATE	PLACE	TIME	WEATHER	COURT CONDITIONS	
HOME	**LEAGUE**	**SEASON**	**OPPONENT**	**LEAGUE**	**SEASON**

SINGLES — RECORDS — MATCH SCORES

No	HOME	H	O	OPPONENT	SET 1	SET 2	SET 3	WINNER
1								
2								
3								
4								
5								
6								

DOUBLES — RECORDS — MATCH SCORES

No	HOME	H	O	OPPONENT	SET 1	SET 2	SET 3	WINNER
1								
2								
3								

TOTALS

TENNIS SCORE SHEET

DATE	PLACE	TIME	WEATHER	COURT CONDITIONS	
HOME	LEAGUE	SEASON	OPPONENT	LEAGUE	SEASON

🎾 SINGLES   RECORDS   MATCH SCORES

No	HOME	H	O	OPPONENT	SET 1	SET 2	SET 3	WINNER
1								
2								
3								
4								
5								
6								

🎾 DOUBLES   RECORDS   MATCH SCORES

No	HOME	H	O	OPPONENT	SET 1	SET 2	SET 3	WINNER
1								
2								
3								

TOTALS

TENNIS SCORE SHEET

DATE	PLACE	TIME	WEATHER	COURT CONDITIONS	
HOME	LEAGUE	SEASON	OPPONENT	LEAGUE	SEASON

SINGLES — RECORDS — MATCH SCORES

No	HOME	H	O	OPPONENT	SET 1	SET 2	SET 3	WINNER
1								
2								
3								
4								
5								
6								

DOUBLES — RECORDS — MATCH SCORES

No	HOME	H	O	OPPONENT	SET 1	SET 2	SET 3	WINNER
1								
2								
3								

TOTALS

TENNIS SCORE SHEET

DATE	PLACE	TIME	WEATHER	COURT CONDITIONS	
HOME	**LEAGUE**	**SEASON**	**OPPONENT**	**LEAGUE**	**SEASON**

SINGLES — RECORDS — MATCH SCORES

No	HOME	H	O	OPPONENT	SET 1	SET 2	SET 3	WINNER
1								
2								
3								
4								
5								
6								

DOUBLES — RECORDS — MATCH SCORES

No	HOME	H	O	OPPONENT	SET 1	SET 2	SET 3	WINNER
1								
2								
3								

TOTALS

TENNIS SCORE SHEET

DATE	PLACE	TIME	WEATHER	COURT CONDITIONS	
HOME	LEAGUE	SEASON	OPPONENT	LEAGUE	SEASON

SINGLES

No	HOME	RECORDS H	RECORDS O	OPPONENT	SET 1	SET 2	SET 3	WINNER
1								
2								
3								
4								
5								
6								

DOUBLES

No	HOME	RECORDS H	RECORDS O	OPPONENT	SET 1	SET 2	SET 3	WINNER
1								
2								
3								

TOTALS			

TENNIS SCORE SHEET

DATE	PLACE	TIME	WEATHER	COURT CONDITIONS	

HOME	LEAGUE	SEASON	OPPONENT	LEAGUE	SEASON

SINGLES · RECORDS · MATCH SCORES

No	HOME	H	O	OPPONENT	SET 1	SET 2	SET 3	WINNER
1								
2								
3								
4								
5								
6								

DOUBLES · RECORDS · MATCH SCORES

No	HOME	H	O	OPPONENT	SET 1	SET 2	SET 3	WINNER
1								
2								
3								

TOTALS

TENNIS SCORE SHEET

DATE	PLACE	TIME	WEATHER	COURT CONDITIONS	
HOME	LEAGUE	SEASON	OPPONENT	LEAGUE	SEASON

SINGLES		RECORDS			MATCH SCORES			
No	HOME	H	O	OPPONENT	SET 1	SET 2	SET 3	WINNER
1								
2								
3								
4								
5								
6								

DOUBLES		RECORDS			MATCH SCORES			
No	HOME	H	O	OPPONENT	SET 1	SET 2	SET 3	WINNER
1								
2								
3								

TOTALS

TENNIS SCORE SHEET

DATE	PLACE	TIME	WEATHER	COURT CONDITIONS	

HOME	LEAGUE	SEASON	OPPONENT	LEAGUE	SEASON

SINGLES · RECORDS · MATCH SCORES

No	HOME	H	O	OPPONENT	SET 1	SET 2	SET 3	WINNER
1								
2								
3								
4								
5								
6								

DOUBLES · RECORDS · MATCH SCORES

No	HOME	H	O	OPPONENT	SET 1	SET 2	SET 3	WINNER
1								
2								
3								

TOTALS

TENNIS SCORE SHEET

DATE	PLACE	TIME	WEATHER	COURT CONDITIONS	

HOME	LEAGUE	SEASON	OPPONENT	LEAGUE	SEASON

SINGLES		RECORDS			MATCH SCORES			
No	**HOME**	**H**	**O**	**OPPONENT**	**SET 1**	**SET 2**	**SET 3**	**WINNER**
1								
2								
3								
4								
5								
6								

DOUBLES		RECORDS			MATCH SCORES			
No	**HOME**	**H**	**O**	**OPPONENT**	**SET 1**	**SET 2**	**SET 3**	**WINNER**
1								
2								
3								

| | | | | | **TOTALS** | | | |

TENNIS SCORE SHEET

DATE	PLACE	TIME	WEATHER	COURT CONDITIONS	
HOME	LEAGUE	SEASON	OPPONENT	LEAGUE	SEASON

SINGLES

No	HOME	H	O	OPPONENT	SET 1	SET 2	SET 3	WINNER
1								
2								
3								
4								
5								
6								

RECORDS   MATCH SCORES

DOUBLES

No	HOME	H	O	OPPONENT	SET 1	SET 2	SET 3	WINNER
1								
2								
3								

RECORDS   MATCH SCORES

TOTALS

TENNIS SCORE SHEET

DATE	PLACE	TIME	WEATHER	COURT CONDITIONS	
HOME	LEAGUE	SEASON	OPPONENT	LEAGUE	SEASON

SINGLES — RECORDS — MATCH SCORES

No	HOME	H	O	OPPONENT	SET 1	SET 2	SET 3	WINNER
1								
2								
3								
4								
5								
6								

DOUBLES — RECORDS — MATCH SCORES

No	HOME	H	O	OPPONENT	SET 1	SET 2	SET 3	WINNER
1								
2								
3								

TOTALS

TENNIS SCORE SHEET

DATE	PLACE	TIME	WEATHER	COURT CONDITIONS	
HOME	**LEAGUE**	**SEASON**	**OPPONENT**	**LEAGUE**	**SEASON**

SINGLES — RECORDS — MATCH SCORES

No	HOME	H	O	OPPONENT	SET 1	SET 2	SET 3	WINNER
1								
2								
3								
4								
5								
6								

DOUBLES — RECORDS — MATCH SCORES

No	HOME	H	O	OPPONENT	SET 1	SET 2	SET 3	WINNER
1								
2								
3								

TOTALS

TENNIS SCORE SHEET

DATE	PLACE	TIME	WEATHER	COURT CONDITIONS	
HOME	LEAGUE	SEASON	OPPONENT	LEAGUE	SEASON

🎾 SINGLES — RECORDS — MATCH SCORES

No	HOME	H	O	OPPONENT	SET 1	SET 2	SET 3	WINNER
1								
2								
3								
4								
5								
6								

🎾 DOUBLES — RECORDS — MATCH SCORES

No	HOME	H	O	OPPONENT	SET 1	SET 2	SET 3	WINNER
1								
2								
3								

	TOTALS			

TENNIS SCORE SHEET

DATE	PLACE	TIME	WEATHER	COURT CONDITIONS	
HOME	**LEAGUE**	**SEASON**	**OPPONENT**	**LEAGUE**	**SEASON**

SINGLES — RECORDS — MATCH SCORES

No	HOME	H	O	OPPONENT	SET 1	SET 2	SET 3	WINNER
1								
2								
3								
4								
5								
6								

DOUBLES — RECORDS — MATCH SCORES

No	HOME	H	O	OPPONENT	SET 1	SET 2	SET 3	WINNER
1								
2								
3								

TOTALS

TENNIS SCORE SHEET

DATE	PLACE	TIME	WEATHER	COURT CONDITIONS	
HOME	**LEAGUE**	**SEASON**	**OPPONENT**	**LEAGUE**	**SEASON**

SINGLES   RECORDS   MATCH SCORES

No	HOME	H	O	OPPONENT	SET 1	SET 2	SET 3	WINNER
1								
2								
3								
4								
5								
6								

DOUBLES   RECORDS   MATCH SCORES

No	HOME	H	O	OPPONENT	SET 1	SET 2	SET 3	WINNER
1								
2								
3								

TOTALS

TENNIS SCORE SHEET

DATE	PLACE	TIME	WEATHER	COURT CONDITIONS	
HOME	LEAGUE	SEASON	OPPONENT	LEAGUE	SEASON

SINGLES

No	HOME	RECORDS		OPPONENT	MATCH SCORES			
		H	O		SET 1	SET 2	SET 3	WINNER
1								
2								
3								
4								
5								
6								

DOUBLES

No	HOME	RECORDS		OPPONENT	MATCH SCORES			
		H	O		SET 1	SET 2	SET 3	WINNER
1								
2								
3								

TOTALS

TENNIS SCORE SHEET

DATE	PLACE	TIME	WEATHER	COURT CONDITIONS	
HOME	LEAGUE	SEASON	OPPONENT	LEAGUE	SEASON

SINGLES — RECORDS — MATCH SCORES

No	HOME	H	O	OPPONENT	SET 1	SET 2	SET 3	WINNER
1								
2								
3								
4								
5								
6								

DOUBLES — RECORDS — MATCH SCORES

No	HOME	H	O	OPPONENT	SET 1	SET 2	SET 3	WINNER
1								
2								
3								

TOTALS

TENNIS SCORE SHEET

DATE	PLACE	TIME	WEATHER	COURT CONDITIONS	
HOME	LEAGUE	SEASON	OPPONENT	LEAGUE	SEASON

SINGLES

No	HOME	RECORDS H	RECORDS O	OPPONENT	SET 1	SET 2	SET 3	WINNER
1								
2								
3								
4								
5								
6								

DOUBLES

No	HOME	RECORDS H	RECORDS O	OPPONENT	SET 1	SET 2	SET 3	WINNER
1								
2								
3								

TOTALS

TENNIS SCORE SHEET

DATE	PLACE	TIME	WEATHER	COURT CONDITIONS	
HOME	LEAGUE	SEASON	OPPONENT	LEAGUE	SEASON

🎾 SINGLES — RECORDS / MATCH SCORES

No	HOME	H	O	OPPONENT	SET 1	SET 2	SET 3	WINNER
1								
2								
3								
4								
5								
6								

🎾 DOUBLES — RECORDS / MATCH SCORES

No	HOME	H	O	OPPONENT	SET 1	SET 2	SET 3	WINNER
1								
2								
3								

TOTALS

TENNIS SCORE SHEET

DATE	PLACE	TIME	WEATHER	COURT CONDITIONS	

HOME	LEAGUE	SEASON	OPPONENT	LEAGUE	SEASON

SINGLES

No	HOME	RECORDS		OPPONENT	MATCH SCORES			
		H	O		SET 1	SET 2	SET 3	WINNER
1								
2								
3								
4								
5								
6								

DOUBLES

No	HOME	RECORDS		OPPONENT	MATCH SCORES			
		H	O		SET 1	SET 2	SET 3	WINNER
1								
2								
3								

TOTALS

TENNIS SCORE SHEET

DATE	PLACE	TIME	WEATHER	COURT CONDITIONS	
HOME	LEAGUE	SEASON	OPPONENT	LEAGUE	SEASON

SINGLES · RECORDS · MATCH SCORES

No	HOME	H	O	OPPONENT	SET 1	SET 2	SET 3	WINNER
1								
2								
3								
4								
5								
6								

DOUBLES · RECORDS · MATCH SCORES

No	HOME	H	O	OPPONENT	SET 1	SET 2	SET 3	WINNER
1								
2								
3								

TOTALS

TENNIS SCORE SHEET

DATE	PLACE	TIME	WEATHER	COURT CONDITIONS	
HOME	LEAGUE	SEASON	OPPONENT	LEAGUE	SEASON

SINGLES		RECORDS			MATCH SCORES			
No	HOME	H	O	OPPONENT	SET 1	SET 2	SET 3	WINNER
1								
2								
3								
4								
5								
6								

DOUBLES		RECORDS			MATCH SCORES			
No	HOME	H	O	OPPONENT	SET 1	SET 2	SET 3	WINNER
1								
2								
3								

	TOTALS		

TENNIS SCORE SHEET

DATE	PLACE	TIME	WEATHER	COURT CONDITIONS	
HOME	LEAGUE	SEASON	OPPONENT	LEAGUE	SEASON

SINGLES — RECORDS — MATCH SCORES

No	HOME	H	O	OPPONENT	SET 1	SET 2	SET 3	WINNER
1								
2								
3								
4								
5								
6								

DOUBLES — RECORDS — MATCH SCORES

No	HOME	H	O	OPPONENT	SET 1	SET 2	SET 3	WINNER
1								
2								
3								

			TOTALS				

TENNIS SCORE SHEET

DATE	PLACE	TIME	WEATHER	COURT CONDITIONS	
HOME	LEAGUE	SEASON	OPPONENT	LEAGUE	SEASON

SINGLES

No	HOME	RECORDS H	O	OPPONENT	MATCH SCORES SET 1	SET 2	SET 3	WINNER
1								
2								
3								
4								
5								
6								

DOUBLES

No	HOME	RECORDS H	O	OPPONENT	MATCH SCORES SET 1	SET 2	SET 3	WINNER
1								
2								
3								

TOTALS

TENNIS SCORE SHEET

DATE	PLACE	TIME	WEATHER	COURT CONDITIONS	
HOME	**LEAGUE**	**SEASON**	**OPPONENT**	**LEAGUE**	**SEASON**

SINGLES

No	HOME	H	O	OPPONENT	SET 1	SET 2	SET 3	WINNER
1								
2								
3								
4								
5								
6								

RECORDS · MATCH SCORES

DOUBLES

No	HOME	H	O	OPPONENT	SET 1	SET 2	SET 3	WINNER
1								
2								
3								

RECORDS · MATCH SCORES

TOTALS

TENNIS SCORE SHEET

DATE	PLACE	TIME	WEATHER	COURT CONDITIONS	
HOME	**LEAGUE**	**SEASON**	**OPPONENT**	**LEAGUE**	**SEASON**

SINGLES — RECORDS — MATCH SCORES

No	HOME	H	O	OPPONENT	SET 1	SET 2	SET 3	WINNER
1								
2								
3								
4								
5								
6								

DOUBLES — RECORDS — MATCH SCORES

No	HOME	H	O	OPPONENT	SET 1	SET 2	SET 3	WINNER
1								
2								
3								

| | | | | | **TOTALS** | | | |

TENNIS SCORE SHEET

DATE	PLACE	TIME	WEATHER	COURT CONDITIONS	

HOME	LEAGUE	SEASON	OPPONENT	LEAGUE	SEASON

SINGLES

No	HOME	H	O	OPPONENT	SET 1	SET 2	SET 3	WINNER
1								
2								
3								
4								
5								
6								

DOUBLES

No	HOME	H	O	OPPONENT	SET 1	SET 2	SET 3	WINNER
1								
2								
3								

TOTALS

TENNIS SCORE SHEET

DATE	PLACE	TIME	WEATHER	COURT CONDITIONS	
HOME	**LEAGUE**	**SEASON**	**OPPONENT**	**LEAGUE**	**SEASON**

SINGLES

No	HOME	RECORDS H	RECORDS O	OPPONENT	SET 1	SET 2	SET 3	WINNER
1								
2								
3								
4								
5								
6								

RECORDS — **MATCH SCORES**

DOUBLES

No	HOME	RECORDS H	RECORDS O	OPPONENT	SET 1	SET 2	SET 3	WINNER
1								
2								
3								

RECORDS — **MATCH SCORES**

TOTALS

TENNIS SCORE SHEET

DATE	PLACE	TIME	WEATHER	COURT CONDITIONS	
HOME	LEAGUE	SEASON	OPPONENT	LEAGUE	SEASON

SINGLES · RECORDS · MATCH SCORES

No	HOME	H	O	OPPONENT	SET 1	SET 2	SET 3	WINNER
1								
2								
3								
4								
5								
6								

DOUBLES · RECORDS · MATCH SCORES

No	HOME	H	O	OPPONENT	SET 1	SET 2	SET 3	WINNER
1								
2								
3								

TOTALS

TENNIS SCORE SHEET

DATE	PLACE	TIME	WEATHER	COURT CONDITIONS	
HOME	LEAGUE	SEASON	OPPONENT	LEAGUE	SEASON

🎾 SINGLES — RECORDS — MATCH SCORES

No	HOME	H	O	OPPONENT	SET 1	SET 2	SET 3	WINNER
1								
2								
3								
4								
5								
6								

🎾 DOUBLES — RECORDS — MATCH SCORES

No	HOME	H	O	OPPONENT	SET 1	SET 2	SET 3	WINNER
1								
2								
3								

TOTALS

TENNIS SCORE SHEET

DATE	PLACE	TIME	WEATHER	COURT CONDITIONS	
HOME	LEAGUE	SEASON	OPPONENT	LEAGUE	SEASON

SINGLES — RECORDS / MATCH SCORES

No	HOME	H	O	OPPONENT	SET 1	SET 2	SET 3	WINNER
1								
2								
3								
4								
5								
6								

DOUBLES — RECORDS / MATCH SCORES

No	HOME	H	O	OPPONENT	SET 1	SET 2	SET 3	WINNER
1								
2								
3								

TOTALS

TENNIS SCORE SHEET

DATE	PLACE	TIME	WEATHER	COURT CONDITIONS	

HOME	LEAGUE	SEASON	OPPONENT	LEAGUE	SEASON

SINGLES · RECORDS · MATCH SCORES

No	HOME	H	O	OPPONENT	SET 1	SET 2	SET 3	WINNER
1								
2								
3								
4								
5								
6								

DOUBLES · RECORDS · MATCH SCORES

No	HOME	H	O	OPPONENT	SET 1	SET 2	SET 3	WINNER
1								
2								
3								

TOTALS

TENNIS SCORE SHEET

DATE	PLACE	TIME	WEATHER	COURT CONDITIONS	

HOME	LEAGUE	SEASON	OPPONENT	LEAGUE	SEASON

SINGLES

No	HOME	H	O	OPPONENT	SET 1	SET 2	SET 3	WINNER
1								
2								
3								
4								
5								
6								

RECORDS — MATCH SCORES

DOUBLES

No	HOME	H	O	OPPONENT	SET 1	SET 2	SET 3	WINNER
1								
2								
3								

RECORDS — MATCH SCORES

TOTALS

TENNIS SCORE SHEET

DATE	PLACE	TIME	WEATHER	COURT CONDITIONS	
HOME	LEAGUE	SEASON	OPPONENT	LEAGUE	SEASON

🎾 SINGLES — RECORDS — MATCH SCORES

No	HOME	H	O	OPPONENT	SET 1	SET 2	SET 3	WINNER
1								
2								
3								
4								
5								
6								

🎾 DOUBLES — RECORDS — MATCH SCORES

No	HOME	H	O	OPPONENT	SET 1	SET 2	SET 3	WINNER
1								
2								
3								

TOTALS			

TENNIS SCORE SHEET

DATE	PLACE	TIME	WEATHER	COURT CONDITIONS	
HOME	LEAGUE	SEASON	OPPONENT	LEAGUE	SEASON

SINGLES — RECORDS — MATCH SCORES

No	HOME	H	O	OPPONENT	SET 1	SET 2	SET 3	WINNER
1								
2								
3								
4								
5								
6								

DOUBLES — RECORDS — MATCH SCORES

No	HOME	H	O	OPPONENT	SET 1	SET 2	SET 3	WINNER
1								
2								
3								

TOTALS

TENNIS SCORE SHEET

DATE	PLACE	TIME	WEATHER	COURT CONDITIONS	

HOME	LEAGUE	SEASON	OPPONENT	LEAGUE	SEASON

SINGLES — RECORDS — MATCH SCORES

No	HOME	H	O	OPPONENT	SET 1	SET 2	SET 3	WINNER
1								
2								
3								
4								
5								
6								

DOUBLES — RECORDS — MATCH SCORES

No	HOME	H	O	OPPONENT	SET 1	SET 2	SET 3	WINNER
1								
2								
3								

TOTALS

TENNIS SCORE SHEET

DATE	PLACE	TIME	WEATHER	COURT CONDITIONS	
HOME	**LEAGUE**	**SEASON**	**OPPONENT**	**LEAGUE**	**SEASON**

🎾 SINGLES — RECORDS — MATCH SCORES

No	HOME	H	O	OPPONENT	SET 1	SET 2	SET 3	WINNER
1								
2								
3								
4								
5								
6								

🎾 DOUBLES — RECORDS — MATCH SCORES

No	HOME	H	O	OPPONENT	SET 1	SET 2	SET 3	WINNER
1								
2								
3								

TOTALS

TENNIS SCORE SHEET

DATE	PLACE	TIME	WEATHER	COURT CONDITIONS	

HOME	LEAGUE	SEASON	OPPONENT	LEAGUE	SEASON

SINGLES

No	HOME	RECORDS		OPPONENT	MATCH SCORES			
		H	O		SET 1	SET 2	SET 3	WINNER
1								
2								
3								
4								
5								
6								

DOUBLES

No	HOME	RECORDS		OPPONENT	MATCH SCORES			
		H	O		SET 1	SET 2	SET 3	WINNER
1								
2								
3								

TOTALS

TENNIS SCORE SHEET

DATE	PLACE	TIME	WEATHER	COURT CONDITIONS	
HOME	LEAGUE	SEASON	OPPONENT	LEAGUE	SEASON

SINGLES · RECORDS · MATCH SCORES

No	HOME	H	O	OPPONENT	SET 1	SET 2	SET 3	WINNER
1								
2								
3								
4								
5								
6								

DOUBLES · RECORDS · MATCH SCORES

No	HOME	H	O	OPPONENT	SET 1	SET 2	SET 3	WINNER
1								
2								
3								

TOTALS

TENNIS SCORE SHEET

DATE	PLACE	TIME	WEATHER	COURT CONDITIONS	
HOME	LEAGUE	SEASON	OPPONENT	LEAGUE	SEASON

SINGLES — RECORDS — MATCH SCORES

No	HOME	H	O	OPPONENT	SET 1	SET 2	SET 3	WINNER
1								
2								
3								
4								
5								
6								

DOUBLES — RECORDS — MATCH SCORES

No	HOME	H	O	OPPONENT	SET 1	SET 2	SET 3	WINNER
1								
2								
3								

TOTALS

TENNIS SCORE SHEET

DATE	PLACE	TIME	WEATHER	COURT CONDITIONS	
HOME	LEAGUE	SEASON	OPPONENT	LEAGUE	SEASON

SINGLES

		RECORDS			MATCH SCORES			
No	HOME	H	O	OPPONENT	SET 1	SET 2	SET 3	WINNER
1								
2								
3								
4								
5								
6								

DOUBLES

		RECORDS			MATCH SCORES			
No	HOME	H	O	OPPONENT	SET 1	SET 2	SET 3	WINNER
1								
2								
3								

TOTALS

TENNIS SCORE SHEET

DATE	PLACE	TIME	WEATHER	COURT CONDITIONS	

HOME	LEAGUE	SEASON	OPPONENT	LEAGUE	SEASON

SINGLES — RECORDS / MATCH SCORES

No	HOME	H	O	OPPONENT	SET 1	SET 2	SET 3	WINNER
1								
2								
3								
4								
5								
6								

DOUBLES — RECORDS / MATCH SCORES

No	HOME	H	O	OPPONENT	SET 1	SET 2	SET 3	WINNER
1								
2								
3								

TOTALS			

TENNIS SCORE SHEET

DATE	PLACE	TIME	WEATHER	COURT CONDITIONS	
HOME	LEAGUE	SEASON	OPPONENT	LEAGUE	SEASON

SINGLES

No	HOME	H	O	OPPONENT	SET 1	SET 2	SET 3	WINNER
1								
2								
3								
4								
5								
6								

RECORDS — MATCH SCORES

DOUBLES

No	HOME	H	O	OPPONENT	SET 1	SET 2	SET 3	WINNER
1								
2								
3								

RECORDS — MATCH SCORES

TOTALS

TENNIS SCORE SHEET

DATE	PLACE	TIME	WEATHER	COURT CONDITIONS	
HOME	LEAGUE	SEASON	OPPONENT	LEAGUE	SEASON

🎾 SINGLES — RECORDS — MATCH SCORES

No	HOME	H	O	OPPONENT	SET 1	SET 2	SET 3	WINNER
1								
2								
3								
4								
5								
6								

🎾 DOUBLES — RECORDS — MATCH SCORES

No	HOME	H	O	OPPONENT	SET 1	SET 2	SET 3	WINNER
1								
2								
3								

TOTALS

TENNIS SCORE SHEET

DATE	PLACE	TIME	WEATHER	COURT CONDITIONS	
HOME	LEAGUE	SEASON	OPPONENT	LEAGUE	SEASON

SINGLES — RECORDS — MATCH SCORES

No	HOME	H	O	OPPONENT	SET 1	SET 2	SET 3	WINNER
1								
2								
3								
4								
5								
6								

DOUBLES — RECORDS — MATCH SCORES

No	HOME	H	O	OPPONENT	SET 1	SET 2	SET 3	WINNER
1								
2								
3								

TOTALS

TENNIS SCORE SHEET

DATE	PLACE	TIME	WEATHER	COURT CONDITIONS	
HOME	LEAGUE	SEASON	OPPONENT	LEAGUE	SEASON

SINGLES

No	HOME	RECORDS		OPPONENT	MATCH SCORES			
		H	O		SET 1	SET 2	SET 3	WINNER
1								
2								
3								
4								
5								
6								

DOUBLES

No	HOME	RECORDS		OPPONENT	MATCH SCORES			
		H	O		SET 1	SET 2	SET 3	WINNER
1								
2								
3								

	TOTALS			

TENNIS SCORE SHEET

DATE	PLACE	TIME	WEATHER	COURT CONDITIONS	
HOME	LEAGUE	SEASON	OPPONENT	LEAGUE	SEASON

SINGLES — RECORDS — MATCH SCORES

No	HOME	H	O	OPPONENT	SET 1	SET 2	SET 3	WINNER
1								
2								
3								
4								
5								
6								

DOUBLES — RECORDS — MATCH SCORES

No	HOME	H	O	OPPONENT	SET 1	SET 2	SET 3	WINNER
1								
2								
3								

TOTALS

TENNIS SCORE SHEET

DATE	PLACE	TIME	WEATHER	COURT CONDITIONS	

HOME	LEAGUE	SEASON	OPPONENT	LEAGUE	SEASON

SINGLES

No	HOME	H	O	OPPONENT	SET 1	SET 2	SET 3	WINNER
1								
2								
3								
4								
5								
6								

RECORDS — MATCH SCORES

DOUBLES

No	HOME	H	O	OPPONENT	SET 1	SET 2	SET 3	WINNER
1								
2								
3								

RECORDS — MATCH SCORES

TOTALS

TENNIS SCORE SHEET

DATE	PLACE	TIME	WEATHER	COURT CONDITIONS	
HOME	LEAGUE	SEASON	OPPONENT	LEAGUE	SEASON

SINGLES

		RECORDS			MATCH SCORES			
No	HOME	H	O	OPPONENT	SET 1	SET 2	SET 3	WINNER
1								
2								
3								
4								
5								
6								

DOUBLES

		RECORDS			MATCH SCORES			
No	HOME	H	O	OPPONENT	SET 1	SET 2	SET 3	WINNER
1								
2								
3								

TOTALS

TENNIS SCORE SHEET

DATE	PLACE	TIME	WEATHER	COURT CONDITIONS	

HOME	LEAGUE	SEASON	OPPONENT	LEAGUE	SEASON

SINGLES — RECORDS — MATCH SCORES

No	HOME	H	O	OPPONENT	SET 1	SET 2	SET 3	WINNER
1								
2								
3								
4								
5								
6								

DOUBLES — RECORDS — MATCH SCORES

No	HOME	H	O	OPPONENT	SET 1	SET 2	SET 3	WINNER
1								
2								
3								

TOTALS

TENNIS SCORE SHEET

DATE	PLACE	TIME	WEATHER	COURT CONDITIONS	
HOME	LEAGUE	SEASON	OPPONENT	LEAGUE	SEASON

SINGLES — RECORDS — MATCH SCORES

No	HOME	H	O	OPPONENT	SET 1	SET 2	SET 3	WINNER
1								
2								
3								
4								
5								
6								

DOUBLES — RECORDS — MATCH SCORES

No	HOME	H	O	OPPONENT	SET 1	SET 2	SET 3	WINNER
1								
2								
3								

TOTALS

TENNIS SCORE SHEET

DATE	PLACE	TIME	WEATHER	COURT CONDITIONS	

HOME	LEAGUE	SEASON	OPPONENT	LEAGUE	SEASON

SINGLES

No	HOME	RECORDS H	O	OPPONENT	SET 1	SET 2	SET 3	WINNER
1								
2								
3								
4								
5								
6								

DOUBLES

No	HOME	RECORDS H	O	OPPONENT	SET 1	SET 2	SET 3	WINNER
1								
2								
3								

TOTALS

TENNIS SCORE SHEET

DATE	PLACE	TIME	WEATHER	COURT CONDITIONS	

HOME	LEAGUE	SEASON	OPPONENT	LEAGUE	SEASON

SINGLES · RECORDS · MATCH SCORES

No	HOME	H	O	OPPONENT	SET 1	SET 2	SET 3	WINNER
1								
2								
3								
4								
5								
6								

DOUBLES · RECORDS · MATCH SCORES

No	HOME	H	O	OPPONENT	SET 1	SET 2	SET 3	WINNER
1								
2								
3								

TOTALS

TENNIS SCORE SHEET

DATE	PLACE	TIME	WEATHER	COURT CONDITIONS	
HOME	**LEAGUE**	**SEASON**	**OPPONENT**	**LEAGUE**	**SEASON**

SINGLES — RECORDS — MATCH SCORES

No	HOME	H	O	OPPONENT	SET 1	SET 2	SET 3	WINNER
1								
2								
3								
4								
5								
6								

DOUBLES — RECORDS — MATCH SCORES

No	HOME	H	O	OPPONENT	SET 1	SET 2	SET 3	WINNER
1								
2								
3								

TOTALS

TENNIS SCORE SHEET

DATE	PLACE	TIME	WEATHER	COURT CONDITIONS	
HOME	**LEAGUE**	**SEASON**	**OPPONENT**	**LEAGUE**	**SEASON**

SINGLES

No	HOME	RECORDS H	RECORDS O	OPPONENT	SET 1	SET 2	SET 3	WINNER
1								
2								
3								
4								
5								
6								

DOUBLES

No	HOME	RECORDS H	RECORDS O	OPPONENT	SET 1	SET 2	SET 3	WINNER
1								
2								
3								

TOTALS

TENNIS SCORE SHEET

DATE	PLACE	TIME	WEATHER	COURT CONDITIONS	
HOME	LEAGUE	SEASON	OPPONENT	LEAGUE	SEASON

SINGLES

No	HOME	H	O	OPPONENT	SET 1	SET 2	SET 3	WINNER
1								
2								
3								
4								
5								
6								

DOUBLES

No	HOME	H	O	OPPONENT	SET 1	SET 2	SET 3	WINNER
1								
2								
3								

		TOTALS			

TENNIS SCORE SHEET

DATE	PLACE	TIME	WEATHER	COURT CONDITIONS	
HOME	**LEAGUE**	**SEASON**	**OPPONENT**	**LEAGUE**	**SEASON**

SINGLES — RECORDS — MATCH SCORES

No	HOME	H	O	OPPONENT	SET 1	SET 2	SET 3	WINNER
1								
2								
3								
4								
5								
6								

DOUBLES — RECORDS — MATCH SCORES

No	HOME	H	O	OPPONENT	SET 1	SET 2	SET 3	WINNER
1								
2								
3								

| | | | | **TOTALS** | | | | |

TENNIS SCORE SHEET

DATE	PLACE	TIME	WEATHER	COURT CONDITIONS	
HOME	**LEAGUE**	**SEASON**	**OPPONENT**	**LEAGUE**	**SEASON**

SINGLES — RECORDS — MATCH SCORES

No	HOME	H	O	OPPONENT	SET 1	SET 2	SET 3	WINNER
1								
2								
3								
4								
5								
6								

DOUBLES — RECORDS — MATCH SCORES

No	HOME	H	O	OPPONENT	SET 1	SET 2	SET 3	WINNER
1								
2								
3								

TOTALS

TENNIS SCORE SHEET

DATE	PLACE	TIME	WEATHER	COURT CONDITIONS	
HOME	LEAGUE	SEASON	OPPONENT	LEAGUE	SEASON

SINGLES

No	HOME	RECORDS H	RECORDS O	OPPONENT	SET 1	SET 2	SET 3	WINNER
1								
2								
3								
4								
5								
6								

RECORDS — MATCH SCORES

DOUBLES

No	HOME	RECORDS H	RECORDS O	OPPONENT	SET 1	SET 2	SET 3	WINNER
1								
2								
3								

RECORDS — MATCH SCORES

TOTALS

TENNIS SCORE SHEET

DATE	PLACE	TIME	WEATHER	COURT CONDITIONS	
HOME	**LEAGUE**	**SEASON**	**OPPONENT**	**LEAGUE**	**SEASON**

SINGLES · RECORDS · MATCH SCORES

No	HOME	H	O	OPPONENT	SET 1	SET 2	SET 3	WINNER
1								
2								
3								
4								
5								
6								

DOUBLES · RECORDS · MATCH SCORES

No	HOME	H	O	OPPONENT	SET 1	SET 2	SET 3	WINNER
1								
2								
3								

TOTALS

TENNIS SCORE SHEET

DATE	PLACE	TIME	WEATHER	COURT CONDITIONS	
HOME	LEAGUE	SEASON	OPPONENT	LEAGUE	SEASON

SINGLES — RECORDS — MATCH SCORES

No	HOME	H	O	OPPONENT	SET 1	SET 2	SET 3	WINNER
1								
2								
3								
4								
5								
6								

DOUBLES — RECORDS — MATCH SCORES

No	HOME	H	O	OPPONENT	SET 1	SET 2	SET 3	WINNER
1								
2								
3								

TOTALS

TENNIS SCORE SHEET

DATE	PLACE	TIME	WEATHER	COURT CONDITIONS	
HOME	LEAGUE	SEASON	OPPONENT	LEAGUE	SEASON

SINGLES

No	HOME	RECORDS		OPPONENT	MATCH SCORES			
		H	O		SET 1	SET 2	SET 3	WINNER
1								
2								
3								
4								
5								
6								

DOUBLES

No	HOME	RECORDS		OPPONENT	MATCH SCORES			
		H	O		SET 1	SET 2	SET 3	WINNER
1								
2								
3								

TOTALS			

TENNIS SCORE SHEET

DATE	PLACE	TIME	WEATHER	COURT CONDITIONS	
HOME	LEAGUE	SEASON	OPPONENT	LEAGUE	SEASON

SINGLES

No	HOME	H	O	OPPONENT	SET 1	SET 2	SET 3	WINNER
		RECORDS				MATCH SCORES		
1								
2								
3								
4								
5								
6								

DOUBLES

No	HOME	H	O	OPPONENT	SET 1	SET 2	SET 3	WINNER
		RECORDS				MATCH SCORES		
1								
2								
3								

TOTALS

TENNIS SCORE SHEET

DATE	PLACE	TIME	WEATHER	COURT CONDITIONS	
HOME	LEAGUE	SEASON	OPPONENT	LEAGUE	SEASON

🏸 SINGLES — RECORDS — MATCH SCORES

No	HOME	H	O	OPPONENT	SET 1	SET 2	SET 3	WINNER
1								
2								
3								
4								
5								
6								

🏸 DOUBLES — RECORDS — MATCH SCORES

No	HOME	H	O	OPPONENT	SET 1	SET 2	SET 3	WINNER
1								
2								
3								

TOTALS

TENNIS SCORE SHEET

DATE	PLACE	TIME	WEATHER	COURT CONDITIONS	
HOME	**LEAGUE**	**SEASON**	**OPPONENT**	**LEAGUE**	**SEASON**

SINGLES — RECORDS — MATCH SCORES

No	HOME	H	O	OPPONENT	SET 1	SET 2	SET 3	WINNER
1								
2								
3								
4								
5								
6								

DOUBLES — RECORDS — MATCH SCORES

No	HOME	H	O	OPPONENT	SET 1	SET 2	SET 3	WINNER
1								
2								
3								

			TOTALS		

TENNIS SCORE SHEET

DATE	PLACE	TIME	WEATHER	COURT CONDITIONS	
HOME	**LEAGUE**	**SEASON**	**OPPONENT**	**LEAGUE**	**SEASON**

SINGLES | RECORDS | MATCH SCORES

No	HOME	H	O	OPPONENT	SET 1	SET 2	SET 3	WINNER
1								
2								
3								
4								
5								
6								

DOUBLES | RECORDS | MATCH SCORES

No	HOME	H	O	OPPONENT	SET 1	SET 2	SET 3	WINNER
1								
2								
3								

TOTALS

TENNIS SCORE SHEET

DATE	PLACE	TIME	WEATHER	COURT CONDITIONS	
HOME	LEAGUE	SEASON	OPPONENT	LEAGUE	SEASON

SINGLES

No	HOME	RECORDS H	O	OPPONENT	SET 1	SET 2	SET 3	WINNER
1								
2								
3								
4								
5								
6								

DOUBLES

No	HOME	RECORDS H	O	OPPONENT	SET 1	SET 2	SET 3	WINNER
1								
2								
3								

TOTALS

TENNIS SCORE SHEET

DATE	PLACE	TIME	WEATHER	COURT CONDITIONS	
HOME	**LEAGUE**	**SEASON**	**OPPONENT**	**LEAGUE**	**SEASON**

🎾 SINGLES — RECORDS — MATCH SCORES

No	HOME	H	O	OPPONENT	SET 1	SET 2	SET 3	WINNER
1								
2								
3								
4								
5								
6								

🎾 DOUBLES — RECORDS — MATCH SCORES

No	HOME	H	O	OPPONENT	SET 1	SET 2	SET 3	WINNER
1								
2								
3								

TOTALS

TENNIS SCORE SHEET

DATE	PLACE	TIME	WEATHER	COURT CONDITIONS	
HOME	LEAGUE	SEASON	OPPONENT	LEAGUE	SEASON

SINGLES

No	HOME	H	O	OPPONENT	SET 1	SET 2	SET 3	WINNER
1								
2								
3								
4								
5								
6								

RECORDS · MATCH SCORES

DOUBLES

No	HOME	H	O	OPPONENT	SET 1	SET 2	SET 3	WINNER
1								
2								
3								

RECORDS · MATCH SCORES

TOTALS

TENNIS SCORE SHEET

DATE	PLACE	TIME	WEATHER	COURT CONDITIONS	
HOME	**LEAGUE**	**SEASON**	**OPPONENT**	**LEAGUE**	**SEASON**

SINGLES

No	HOME	H	O	OPPONENT	SET 1	SET 2	SET 3	WINNER
1								
2								
3								
4								
5								
6								

RECORDS — MATCH SCORES

DOUBLES

No	HOME	H	O	OPPONENT	SET 1	SET 2	SET 3	WINNER
1								
2								
3								

RECORDS — MATCH SCORES

TOTALS

TENNIS SCORE SHEET

DATE	PLACE	TIME	WEATHER	COURT CONDITIONS	
HOME	**LEAGUE**	**SEASON**	**OPPONENT**	**LEAGUE**	**SEASON**

SINGLES

No	HOME	H	O	OPPONENT	SET 1	SET 2	SET 3	WINNER
1								
2								
3								
4								
5								
6								

RECORDS — MATCH SCORES

DOUBLES

No	HOME	H	O	OPPONENT	SET 1	SET 2	SET 3	WINNER
1								
2								
3								

RECORDS — MATCH SCORES

TOTALS

TENNIS SCORE SHEET

DATE	PLACE	TIME	WEATHER	COURT CONDITIONS	
HOME	LEAGUE	SEASON	OPPONENT	LEAGUE	SEASON

SINGLES — RECORDS — MATCH SCORES

No	HOME	H	O	OPPONENT	SET 1	SET 2	SET 3	WINNER
1								
2								
3								
4								
5								
6								

DOUBLES — RECORDS — MATCH SCORES

No	HOME	H	O	OPPONENT	SET 1	SET 2	SET 3	WINNER
1								
2								
3								

TOTALS

TENNIS SCORE BOOK

Are you enjoying this awesome book?

If so, please leave us a review. We are very interested in your feedback to create even better products for you to enjoy soon.

Shopping for Tennis Score Books can be fun. Go to our page on Amazon http://bit.ly/amazing-notebooks or scan the QR code below to see all of our awesome and creative products!

Thank you very much!

Amazing Tennis Score Books
www.amazing-notebooks.com

Made in the USA
Coppell, TX
29 July 2022